The Mission of Addition

To my brother Mike,
the numbers guy in our family
—B.P.C.

Addition:
Combining two
or more numbers
to come up
with their total

The Mission of Addition

by Brian P. Cleary

illustrated by Brian Gable

SCHOLASTIC INC.

New York Toronto London Auckland Sydney
Mexico City New Delhi Hong Kong Buenos Aires

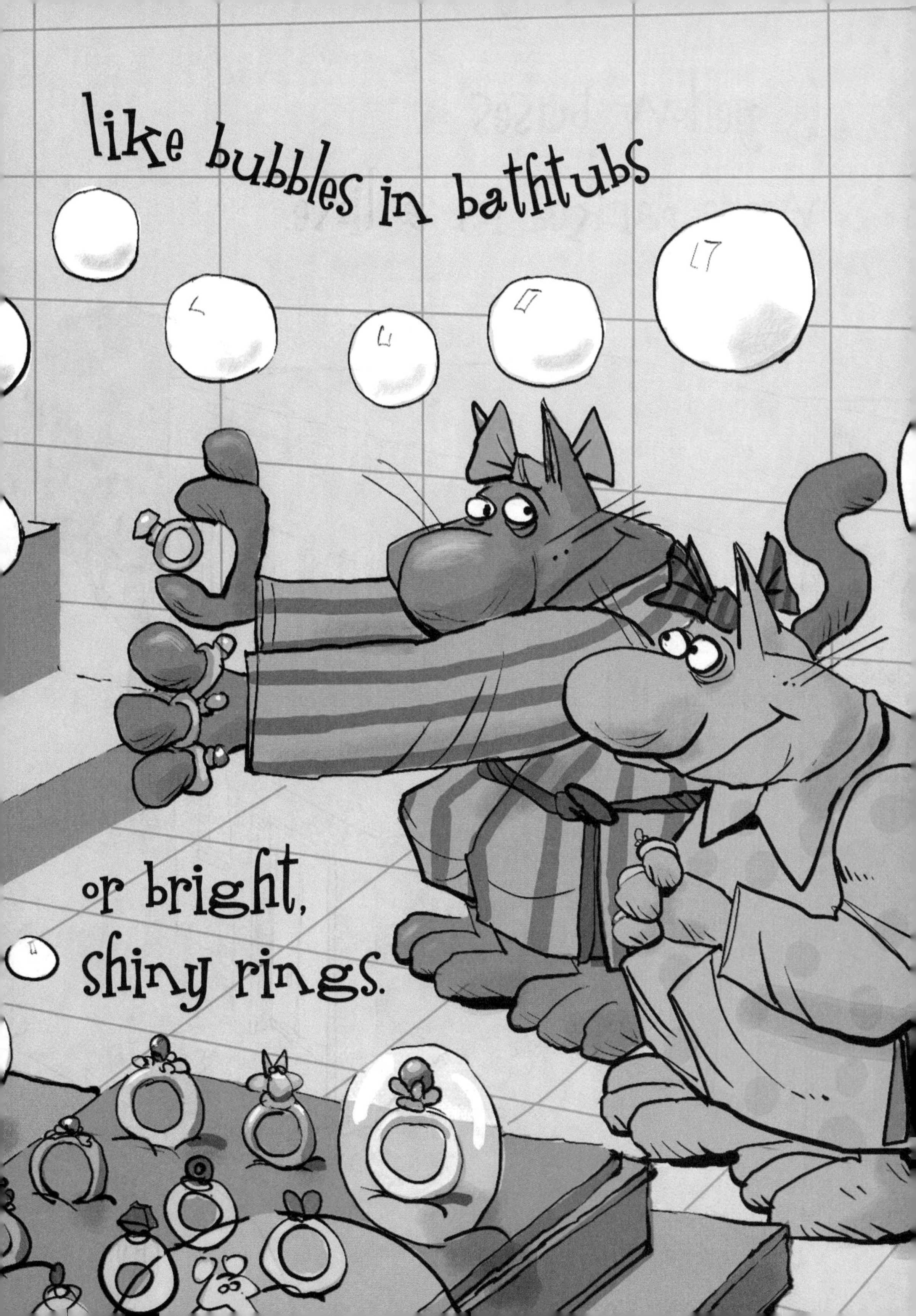

like bubbles in bathtubs

or bright,
shiny rings.

6 yellow buses were parked in a line.

3 pulled behind them,
and then there were 9.

To **add** is to make bigger
the total number of
whatever you are counting up,

like baseballs in a glove.

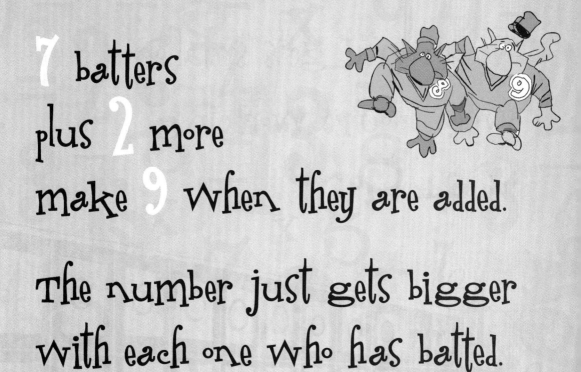

7 batters
plus 2 more
make 9 when they are added.

The number just gets bigger
with each one who has batted.

No amount gets smaller when you're working in **addition**.

The numbers climb from low to high, 'cause that's addition's mission!

The Johnsons had 1 babysitter.

Gretchen was her name.

She cried "Help!"

So, number 2, Miss Higgenbottom, came.

So far,
this made 4 who tried
to keep them all in line.

5th was
Caitlyn MacNamee,

and 6th was Mr. Lee,
and 4 more
totaled 10 in all
to watch that crew of 3.

You see,
to **add** means to **increase**.
It's a way of showing more,

whether counting babysitters

or bread crusts on the floor.

"Plus" can be used
just like "and."
It helps us
when we count,

combining all the numbers
till we get
the full amount.

So, if a hen lays 7 eggs
plus 3,
plus 4,
plus 10,
the total equals 24....

and **1** exhausted hen!

In counting the musicians
in the marching band at school,
you add up all the players
from each group.

Just look, it's cool!

9 are playing trumpet,
plus 3 are on trombone.
2 more jam on flügelhorn
and 6 on saxophone.

When you add 8
bass drummers in,
that equals 28.

So, when it comes to counting,
don't worry, fret, or fuss.

You'll find that knowing how to **add**

is very much a **plus!**

Do you know?

ISBN-13: 978-0-545-03770-9
ISBN-10: 0-545-03770-0

Text copyright © 2005 by Brian P. Cleary.
Illustrations copyright © 2005 by Brian Gable. All rights reserved.
Published by Scholastic Inc., 557 Broadway, New York, NY 10012, by arrangement with Millbrook Press Inc., a division of Lerner Publishing Group. SCHOLASTIC and associated logos are trademarks and/or registered trademarks of Scholastic Inc.

12 11 10 9 8 7 6 5   9 10 11 12/0

Printed in the U.S.A.   23

First Scholastic printing, October 2007